*Pulling at the cords of gender's curtains, watchful of the slipping ~ ,
masks,* with your chest *is a luminously generous and vulnerable debut from Remi
Graves. Their poems do justice to the failures and violences of category and yet –
thirsting for more than this – are courageous enough to refuse to rest there. In a spirit
of playfulness, of childhood, of starlings, Graves's poems glance towards the edges from
which we leap, attentive not to where we might land, but to how we might take flight.*

Victoria Adukwei Bulley

Reading with your chest, *I'm most dazzled by Remi Graves's restless, inventive
imagination. Through linguistic and formal transformations, we follow a speaker
wrestling with the mind's capacity for harm and consolation. Graves understands the
pleasure and power of fantasising, summoning boxers and cockapoos, Spiderman and
Lisa Bonet in these meditations on desire, race, and the body. Pick up this pamphlet, you
too will feel the fantasy.*

Derrick Austin

'where do you go / to write a body' *sets forth the speaker at the beginning of Remi
Graves's beautifully crafted series of poems. What follows is a mesmeric exploration
of betweenness and queer longing; a candid mode of pondering upon the embodied
experience of trans navigation with the world, of conditioned adaptation to the threat
of existing –* 'I hear them ask almost through gritted teeth / are we men?' *A facet
of what makes Graves's lines so impactful is their kaleidoscopic observation towards
the potential of an actualised self; of the speaker, the animals and individuals they
witness; and its limitations in practice –* 'but you don't / know not to look at a ghost
/ unless you can see it'. *I really related to and loved this pamphlet, which so assuredly
announced Graves as a vital voice in poetry. Their astute reflections on gender, race, and
the attractions that move us will stay with me.*

Peter Scalpello

First published in 2022 by Fourteen Publishing.
fourteenpoems.com

Design and typeset by Stromberg Design.
strombergdesign.co.uk

Proofreading and copy editing by Lara Kavanagh.
lk-copy.com

Printed by Print2Demand Ltd, Westoning, Bedfordshire, UK.

Remi Graves has asserted their right to be identified as the author of this work in accordance with the Copyright, Designs and Patents Act 1988.

ISBN:
978-1-8383943-9-4

with your chest

Remi Graves

'There are no opposite shores. We are always at the crossing of paths'
Paul B. Preciado

contents:

untitled

where do you go
to write a body—

              bones dislocated by the audacious
              flesh pink rubber on the tip

                          of the world's pencil
                          skin pushed into meaning

always and only ever meaning.
lynched on the pin of a semantic field

                        you never were asked to pick.

where do you go
to wright a body?

              when you would rather not
              speak of the dismembered and re-membered flesh

                        floating about in your head.

where do you go
to right a body wronged—

              bend it into being
              Lazarise it out of signifying,

                      out of the aching invisible

 into light.

here at the shore

not of myself
or the earth
or the air
with lungs ablaze
the body a flame
I could say something
is happening
or about to
above a plane rips through the clouds
puffed as if from the lash of a whip
and just like that, scar tissue hovers
over our lives untended to
altering the curve and taste
of all this living
an unlicked wound
but hear at the shore
not of time or change
or what could be possible
there are bubbles in the blood
and birds flocking to somewhere safer
which means
it must exist?

spiderman

can you hurtle
towards something
at a snail's pace? I have
always at once been in a rush
with my feet slammed on the brakes.
My tall friend asks me to s l o w   d o w n
as we walk towards the station, the shops, anywhere
but ourselves. I joke that one of their steps equals five of mine,
that I'm hurrying to keep up with them which is only partially untrue
maybe i'm running scared of who will catch up with me if I do relax: the stubbled, muscled,
manned version of me whose yearning for I barely let myself imagine, apart from as a small
child loving my spiderman figurine more than any real thing   his plastic chest, ripped,
polished, his cinched waist, the fantasy of slicing through air too fast, oh to be
a boy and a blur— if I were to let up, slow my roll and we bumped
into each other, fantasy me and me, because he has always been
there, at my heels, and if he were to grab me gently to stop
us falling to the ground   what would I do then,
held in my own arms, stopped dead
in the middle of the street by who
I've always wanted to be,
who I could have
if I'd only had
a taste for—
what's the
opposite of
speed?

8

at bay

I may have held myself there for too long,
as though I were an army advancing on
enemy territory   but also at bay like
in the harbour, lost at sea, floating, drowning
or dead in the way people scared of living live.
kept at bay as in: don't let it out, fight that off.
it's hard to say where I went in the keeping,
I was not only hovering at my own shore all those years
I visited others, helped with their own private wars:
one way to escape the soft-shelled cage of your own
body   well I did and I didn't   all I know is eventually
I awoke kneeled in a corner unable to move closer
to myself— but wanting to for once— and all
of this has something to do with the shape
made of me by others— dogs baying
at a deer trying to live without fight—
but more so to do with knowing myself,
and the world, well enough to understand
I had things to hide
little pearls of feeling and want
that I knew to turn away from
even when they blossomed me
fragrant
iridescent
aglow

prénom

I never realised
how much I love my name
which is a boy's in french
and anyone's in Yorùbá;

was a sign, a song
telling me who I was

that I liked being anyone
in one tongue
and a boy in another
watching my shape shift
depending on the mouth in charge

I held on to it, my name, for dear life
when the world was not holding me
with any real grip
at least I have this
at least

I would say it backwards
marvel at its timbre,
how it never gave way
to certainty
i m e r i m e r i m e r
I knew I was safe in there
nestled, or at sea, certainly
hard to reach

I have many times given thanks
to my parents for offering it to me
what a comfort
to be seen somehow before arriving.
not to have to rename myself,
but to have the way made for me
to feel that I am as I should be

how did they know who I was
before I got here, what kind
of name someone like me would need
what safety or alarm bell necessary
to usher me through the halls
of this too split place

or did they conjure me up
as I am, in between, beyond,
in the naming
a gift
I didn't need to give myself.

equal opportunities

Which term best represents your gender?

seahorse   seasonal   selectively mute   sassy as I wanna be

snake in the grass   self-proclaimed at birth   on annual leave

other ....

Please select one answer to indicate your ethnicity:

Black/Black British: African

Black/Black British: Caribbean

Mixed/African and Caribbean

Black/get me out of here[1]

Black/let the black security guard follow you round the shop when all you want is a bag of hula hoops, because you don't want him to lose his job

Black/with a white ancestor you don't want to find out more about

Black/looking for another name to call yourself, something from before

Black/staring at your own tongue in the mirror, unsure if it can be trusted to speak for you

Black/brown, magnet to sun and shimmer, get down in the dance, stand up at the protest, walk home get called nigger by the homeless man you were fumbling for a pound for in your pocket

Black/writing the same thing over and and over and

1 promise me there is an elsewhere

12

over and over and over and over and over and over and over and over and over
and over and over and over and over and over and over and over and over and
over and over and over and over and over and over and over and over and over
and over and over and over and over and over and over and over and over and
over and over and over and over and over and over and over and over and over
over and over and over and over and over and over and over and over and over
over and over and over and over and over and over and over and over and over
and over and over and overover and over and over and over and over and over
and over and over and over and over and over and over and over and over and
over and over and over and over and over and voer and over dan over and over
and over and over and over and over and over and over and over and overover
and over and over and over and over and over and over and over and over and
over and over and over and over and over and over and over and over and over
and over and over and over and over and over and over and over and over and
over and over and over and over and overover and over and over and over and
over and over and overandoverandoverandover and over and ovander and vore
nad over and over and over and over and over and over and over and over and
over and over and over and over and over and over and over and overover and
over and over and over and over and over and over and over and over and over
and over and over and over and over and over and over and over and over and
over and over and overover and over and over and over and over and over and
over and over and over and over and over and over and over and over and over
and over and over and over and over and over and over and over and over and
over and over and over and over and over and over and over and overover and
over and over and over and over and over dane reov nad vroe d a n o v e r and over and
over and over and over and over and over and over and over and over and over and over
and over and over and over and over and over and over and over and over and
over and overover and over and over and over and over and over and over and
over and over and over and over and over and over and over and over and over
and over and over and over and over and over and over and over and over and
over and over and over and over and over and over and overover and over and
over and over and over and over and over and over and over dn oaver and over
and over and over and over and over and over and over and over and over and
over and over and over and over da nover and over and over and over and over
and over and over and overover and over and over anever aod over and over
and over and over and over and over and over and over and over and over and
over and over and over and over and over and over and over dan over and reov
and over ad nevorandover adn ovre and over and dao nvre over andov er adn
voer dnva vroe nad evor dan orev and voadr an

pockets

did you know
the body is not a cupboard
not a pocket to be stuffed
like a hungry mouth?
no one told me that—
me the child hovering
by the table at parties
scoffing as many unwarmed
sausage rolls into my mouth
before hometime
because we weren't allowed such treats
and I knew myself well enough— back then
to understand what I wanted
and liked myself enough
to give in to my desire
when I could

at the bar

I used to watch in awe
Papa at the pull up bar
between the living room
and corridor, mesmerised
by the tectonic plates of his back.
muscle converging at a glacial pace,
me admiring— which in all of us, but in
children especially, is a kind of wishing—
his body   the slow shift and hover
as he pulled himself   up   up
such control, moving against
whatever mean spirited whisper
kept him stuck in most ways
other than the body, moving
to whatever music in the muscle

here at the gay bar, I am again in awe
and afraid of the man who seas me
eyes unfogged by the world's
misty rumours, raises in me
with his gaze the masculine urge
to—
like a tide that pulls me to myself
yet insists I do not speak
lest I break the spell
with the timbre of my own
unbroken voice, Papa
I too am shaking
pulled into fear
by what buoys me up

lout

say someone stares / for long enough / am i allowed to snap / a photo of their face / taking me in / capture the capturing / the cage of their gaze / I nearly did today / the man on the bench with the five o'clock shadow / eyes that looked like punching was the only way he knew how to ask a question / he looked and looked without smiling / a face like stone / like he was digging for the thing he was afraid of / that someone other / could do man as well as him / with no chin hair to prove it / his stare a shovel trying to root out the seed / of what he recognised in me / and I nearly swung the camera from behind my back / how boxers swing arms / round and into my hands / nearly pressed the shutter button like the trigger of a bulletless gun / the flash hitting his face like cold water / or a fist / to bring him back into his own body / out of mine / really i just stared back for a few seconds / blank despite the ache in my chest[1] / all i could muster not actually knowing how to fight / and not knowing if he knew I was not a threat / and still in walking on / I doubted what I had seen / stopped myself turning back to check / wondered if the metal glint of an arrow i glimpsed in his eyes / was ever there at all / his searching look a weapon formed against me / or if in fact all the drama of disgust was mine alone / an imaginary shard / and if the photo once looked at would show nothing / but an open landscape of a face / threat-less / unperturbed by me / invisible daytime ghost of gender / and what if I had drawn in the hostility / with my own crayon fear of men and what they see in me / or what i long for in them

1 is this what he recognised?

face off

I've found my latest obsession / the bit just after the weigh in before a boxing match / I'm much too soft to watch / the ballet of men punching each other / wherever the body will allow / but the intense glaring at one and other / from the safety of their own frames / I back it / the leaning in so close they can taste the breath of the other on their lips / the hoping / the wondering how they don't just kiss / I can't get enough / I considered making some kind of video art piece about it / my friend suggested I should / but here we are / in the flat world / talking instead of doing / which is what they're up to / angry whispering sweet nothings / want swelling up their chests / the sometimes rush of expletives / the negs / in one of these videos the taller guy actually winks and puckers his lips / this / is / hot / I turn the volume right down / to hear the straight up dirty talk simmering in the subtext / sometimes I do my own lipsync / make them say what I want / it's the drama for me / the stilted dance of two guys squaring up / for the benefit of us / the circling around what the whole world is scared of / it's a scam they might shout at the top of their swollen lungs / we're actually in love / I imagine this each time / laughing to myself / crying for joy / wishing for one of them to lean his head into the other's chest / in the clinch / lie it there for a while as he heaves / sweat pouring / as though the heavens have parted / just for this / just so they might leave themselves open enough to

chasing light

waiting for water to return
to this stretched shore, we catch

flickers of a murmuration, starlings,
blurred on the blade of the horizon,

climbing air: an orchestra of feather and bone
weaving in and out of wind—

they dive, and for a second the sky is empty,
then volta, full of flutter— light, an allegro

on this body of birds rising
into the dance of the disappearing;

beside you, new love, a cold tide seeps,
bears witness to the fugue, that speaks

of how they trust the air enough
to fall.

the birds are flocking again

then playing at landing
on a sloping roof   tiptoeing
down its incline

before one of them launches
itself into the sky
as if it were a magnet

knowing the others will follow.
damn those pigeons,
their winged confidence

and the spider in the garden is at it too
shifting its slim heft
down the line of its web

legs wide, gleeful
is this faith?

what do they know that we don't
about leaping
what is below

the (un)godly timing of things

in the morning of a life

the sun is early in the sky
there is enough light

to lay out the necessary things,
to set some small pebbles down

on the paths we'll take and chalk
for making note of all the firsts

first gust of wind, first scent
of lavender crushed, first after first

until in the mourning of a life
which for the sake of this we'll call night

we face what couldn't last
in the backroom of grandma's house

we arrange what's been left behind
sort through who'll take what

a cruel auction where no one gets
what they are really bidding for

(her to come back
from her disappearing act

or at least a map for how she might be reached)
we lay out the things she's touched

though I don't know if a soul can be laid
if it can be hung up at an altar

spread across a table with other knick knacks
like this bird-shaped paperweight

that I never once looked at when she was here
but now sits on my record player

nothing of her in its clear glass,
not a memory, or a loose association and yet

its weight does something
my palm a little heavier in the holding

my heart not a featherbone lighter
even though I am trying to let go

children know what they like

no one can tell me otherwise.
I used to babysit Christophe
who loved the stretch of
washing up gloves, the leather
straps of his school shoes,
buckles and belts,
would tell us all about it at dinner
because he didn't know
yet, who he could trust
how shame turns
all flavour to dust

at six years old

when Lisa Bonet's face
casts its light skin shadow
across your TV screen,
when the only way you could imagine
your skins touching
was with you dipped in a chalk
and in this baptism you dropped
the innate feminine
grew a thing between your legs
to ratify your desire
built a town across your shoulders
broad and there enough to sustain you
a small black thing wanting
to love lightie mclight like blondie mcblonde.
Young enough to think the world sees you
how you see yourself, old enough to flick
the channel quick when your mother walks in.
You, the small black thing playing
with your three selves,
before knowing any of their names.

paracetamol

the sheets bunched around you like a ~~life~~
straight jacket. you're tossing and turning
on sleep's ship in choppy waters
slow aching cramps spread how a bad
smell does, or a lie, and pain can be truth
dropped into you like a blood clot in the bowl.
paracetamol or agony, transition or be forever
questioning if less, if this, is enough.
you to and fro longing for the cold side of the pill-
ow, like it's an opposite country and everywhere
lukewarm is here. give in, reach for the drugs,
cut your thumb fumbling with the foil,
suck your injured finger, stunned to sleep by
the clarity of this mid-night dispatch

strong

To grip your hips as you bend, opening the oven—
to press myself not quite into you, but close—
is to know exactly who I want
and still be shadow-boxing such muscular lust.

I grapple with the thought of holding you tighter.
In the midday light, when it is impossible not to glimpse
the tree trunk shadow I imagine my body casting over yours
when I am just a branch, made strong by what is heavy:
the guilt of wanting you the way they say men do.

I'd like to shut my eyes like you do,
let them roll back into silence and feeling,
swap the fears I have yet to name for
the taste of skin, lips and shared breath.

You pull the oven door shut.
I am still in awe
of the way you trap heat.

outrageous

it's true, I have gone a whole day
without using the bathroom
for fear of being refused entry
at the door, so it's almost cruel
watching from the bench opposite—
outside this library whose toilets
leave me petrified and swollen—
as a white woman's cockapoo pisses
on a black man's leather bag
which he'd put down whilst
chatting on the phone
to what could be a cousin
or a close friend. I watch on
in disbelief, the bulge of my bladder
begging for relief whilst
the white woman wipes
furiously at the man's soiled
satchel, crouched at his feet,
apologising to the air,
she mops, the tissue in her hand
barely soaking up anything
at all.

pissing

after Andrew McMillan

on tiptoes
legs akimbo
practising what I'd observed
then tried to learn by heart:
what my father and brother shared
at the bowl, how they stood
bold, their backs to the world
so why shouldn't I
the world already having turned
its back on me.
I'm hovering over its gaping mouth
giddy with the knowledge that this is not
how *I* should do it,
heart rattling in its cage
a thrill even behind the locked door
no one knowing what I'm up to, not even me,
I make a mess, it trickles down my legs,
speckles the seat, which I don't know to lift,
all of this aiming my stream
without a thing to direct it,
pissing in the wind
all wound up,
aren't you meant to wee on the wound
to alleviate the sting?
who would want to sit
with that kind of thing
when you could stand above it
look down at what is leaking out
from enough distance to think
you might be able
to run from it
at any given moment,
always ready to run.

outrun

the dark sky is an invisibility cloak
a silhouette is just a shape, yet
I'm not sure I won't be run out
of my body tonight, this unisex
thing causing trouble wherever
it goes   my boots tap a dirge
on the pavement   before I know
what is about to happen
a man carving zigzags in the street
approaches, leans towards me as if
I'm a lamppost   an altar
          battiman he slurs
waving a finger in my face so I know
where his tongue is aimed.
I lower my eyes, a clutched fist
in my pocket though I have never punched
anything apart from the air
above me after making a hoop
on the basketball court with other—
          nah battiwoman, you lucky…
          if you was a battiman, I'd fuck you up
eyes down I give him a wide berth
—though the distance may be what's eating at him—
he's behind me now
words garbling the air,
dripping from his mouth
like a dog run ragged, or dying
of thirst.

things men say to me thinking I too, am a man

alright fella?

               this train for cheshunt, boss?

                             thank you brother

so much man in each utterance,
women don't call me sis—
do they know what I am not?—
half as much as men call me man
are they on to me?
or unsure so trying to fasten
certainty where it doesn't exist?
does it ever exist?
I feel them almost ask through gritted teeth
are we men?
is this what we are meant for?
tugging at the seams of respect
reaching for recognition at the altar
of each other—or is it I kneeling
at the altar of them?

contact

we push   the mist
of ourselves into the backs
of necks, the crease of ears
in lamp-kissed darkness
shapes more solid than shadow
          arise out of bed sheets,
offer us a marionette
play of the work we do
under the cover of each other.
Searching for our hearts
     in the bodies of others
we are surgeons to all past lovers,
breaking breastplates with blunt kisses
tonguing   the centre
for a taste of ourselves.
Shelter in the dip of a hip,
a pressed palm on a thigh rising
sultry bodies the shape of all
that was imagined   forbidden
     you, arched at the desk
of my back fold and push
out old ways of being.
Who knew a body could
be used   to parse a life.

streetdance

when walking
behind women

i   s   l   o   w

d   o   w   n

        o
         r
           c
          r
            o
              s
                s
                    t
                   h
                  e
                      r
                     o
                      a
                     d

                         because i have no way
                         to say
                          i am one of them,
                              almost,
                         or have been
                             or if not quite,
                         at least,
                         at best,
                         i am not a threat
                         and actually—*i don't*
                         tell them this—
                         i am also scared,
                         of what a woman

could do in my face
at the threshold
of the public toilet
as my bladder knocks
at the door of my body,
i am punished
for how i look,
what i need.

when walking
        behind men,
i try to overtake

o
r

l
e
t

t
h
e
m

to make sure
we are never side by side
for more than a second,
the danger of building
up a rhythm with a stranger
and god what if our eyes
meet and i smile instead of
whatever indifference or
respect i'm meant to exude
....
        ...   so i speed up

as if invisibility
is a destination
reached

by

faster feet

i've also been known to

s
t
e
p

i
n
t
o

t
h
e
road when an oncoming
white person is looking
everywhere but into my
eyes— I am thin as air:
invisible   but you don't
know not to look at a ghost
unless you can see it— like
they are definitely not going
to make way for me lest i
give them the fear they are
used to conjuring up on sight.
in those moments,
i can't help it,
i have an urge
to give myself
to the open road.

[and what of coming face to face with
                    the ones who have touched
all that is unfixed inside them

                              how do i walk past
               when I want to be seen

                              want to shed my ghost body and reverse the exile
what if I have forgotten   —have I ever known—
how to be in my body with those who already know the language it speaks?
               how to let eyes meet without bracing
                    against what the world has told us about ourselves in every
               goddamn

                              tongue and symbol, image and subliminal.]

is this how everyone feels walking down the street,

                                        clutching a tether in their pocket
                    tying them to their body,
          an anchor
               stopping the leap into the air,

                                        the hoping never to land?

34

Acknowledgements

"chasing light" was helped towards its final form by Jacob Sam-La Rose and first published in Barbican Young Poets Anthology 2017: *An Orchestra of Feathers and Bone*.

"untitled" was first published in *fourteen poems* issue 4.

"contact" was first published in *Whut Zine* issue 1.

The epigraph is taken from Paul B. Preciado's *An Apartment on Uranus: Chronicles of the Crossing* (The MIT Press, 2019).

"here at the shore" was inspired by Paul B. Preciado's *An Apartment on Uranus*, which I came to thanks to Alexander Kelvey.

"strong" was first published in Platypus Press Anthology: *Islands Are But Mountains, New poetry from the United Kingdom* in 2019.

"lout" was first published in *Stand* Volume 19, Issue 4.

Thanks to Jacob Sam-La Rose, Barbican Young Poets, The Roundhouse Poetry Collective, and Toast Poets, where I started learning how to write (like) myself. Thanks to my friends and family who supported me when I said I wanted to be a poet.